# When Sunflowers Speak

*an invitation to contemplation*

*poems by*
Patrick W. Flanigan

*photographs by*
David McQueen

*illustrations by*
Christine Crozier

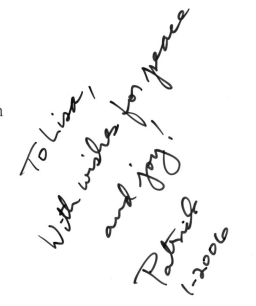

To Lisa !
With wishes for peace
and joy !
Patrick
1-2006

Pacific Grove Publishing

Hand Lettering: Debra Ferreboeuf
Design / Layout: Dave Christensen

Printed in the United States of America
by Cypress Press, Monterey, California


Published by:
Pacific Grove Publishing
P.O. Box 803
Pacific Grove, CA 93950
Telephone: (831) 755-1701
Fax: (831) 375-4749
Email: pgpublishing@redshift.com

1 3 5 7 6 4 2

ISBN 0-9668952-6-6

*Also of interest*
SURVIVING THE STORM
MILK and COFFEE
Poems by
Patrick W. Flanigan

*For my wife, Anita, who loves words, ideas, and family. You are my inspiration.*

*Patrick*

*For my wonderful daughters Kristyn, Karyn and Michelle. And for Sharon. Your love and support have helped me to make it this far.*

*David*

# CONTENTS

# To Write a Poem

You cannot walk
into the garden
and command a poem
to flow from your pen.

It takes time,
the right moment,
joy or hurt,
compassion or anger
to awaken the Muse
that pulls words
out of the cauldron
of language

and places them side by side
and on top of each other
in a leather-bound notebook
or on a corner of a napkin.

Your task is to be there,
awake, seeing, listening,
open to the message
not yet written on the page.

# Listen

Have you ever heard
a muffled voice
like a cry for help
coming from the rubble
of a collapsed building?

Have you ever stopped,
put down the newspaper,
turned off the television,
gone into the garden
and just listened?

Sitting quietly
you might be able
to hear the voice
more clearly.
You might be able
to rescue the soul
buried under the weight
of daily routine.

# The Urge to Travel

What makes you want to travel?

A jet's white trail in the sky,
the whine of tires on a highway,
a ship on the horizon,
a picture of two people
on a sandy beach?

Or are you like me,
one of those who responds
to the low, sad whistle
of a distant train?

Is it the urge to leave
home or office
and see strange lands
or only the wish
to take that trip of childhood
when holding my mother's hand
and hearing her voice
could remove all fear
even on a trembling train
hurtling through the night?

# Driftwood

The bleached trunk
of a once tall tree
rests on a rocky shore
beneath a cliff
topped by cypress
and redwoods.

Months in storm tossed seas
and encounters
with other shores
have stripped away
bark and branches
leaving bare wood,
white and smooth.

The trees above whisper
about the skeleton below.
Some raise their boughs
to heaven in fear and trembling.
Others simply enjoy
the sky, the moist earth,
and the birds
nesting in their branches.

# Not About Trees

This poem is not about trees
although it could be.

It is about people
who stand straight and tall
and those with bent backs
or limbs that have been broken
or lost to disease or accident.

It is about people
with strong, healthy cores
and those who have been made hollow
by hurt or neglect.

It is about people
who support others
with outstretched arms
or give shelter
in the chambers of their hearts.

It is about people
who have been brought down
by unpredictable forces
or consumed by the violence
or passion of others.

And about people
who are firmly attached
to a place by roots
that drink unseen water
from places unknown
to impatient strangers.

This poem is about you
or me or that person over there.
It is not about those trees
that give shade to the playground
and whisper to each other
as a storm approaches.

# The Green of Spring

After months of rain
everything seems new,
fragile, and green.
Blades of grass
cover the meadow,
yellow-green leaves
adorn the trees,
green buds
swell atop stems,
the brick path
is mossy and slick.

But the bark
of the ancient oaks,
pines, and cypress
are not new,
fragile, or green.
They are creviced and wrinkled,
scarred and rough.
They are the brown color
of the rich, moist earth
that, each year,
gives birth
to the bright green
of springtime.

# The Spring Garden

In spring the garden is full of surprises.

Wind blown seeds sprout
in the crevices of brick paths.
Forgotten bulbs push green leaves
and white, blue, and yellow flowers
out of the dark, moist earth.
Skeletal twigs and branches
burst forth with yellow and green leaves
and fragrant pink and white blossoms.
Dark green pines add new pale tufts
to growing branches.

Birds and bugs,
singing and quiet things,
flying and crawling things
share our joy
in the spring garden.

# Scents

The honeysuckle sent
its fragrant perfume
through the crack under the door
awakening him just after dawn.

The garden sought his attention
seducing him
to sink his strong hands
into its moist soil.

He sang softly
gently trimming
and caressing leaves
and stems and blooms.

He worked until dusk
returning to his room,
the scents of a thousand flowers
on his skin.

# The Love Poem

He started to write
a love poem
on the petals
of a daisy.

Not knowing
if she loved him
or loved him not,
he dared
to expose his soul
like the yellow
gold center of the flower
on which he wrote.

Before black ink
stained the last white petal,
she touched his neck
and whispered " I love you".

# The Flowering Tree

In my garden
a certain tree
blooms every summer.
It does not
bear fruit
but covers itself
with more flowers
than there are numbers in the world.

Its joy and generosity
are amazing —
to produce
such beauty
and not have
eyes.

# Patience

Some things cannot be rushed —
the appearance of a shooting star,
the opening of a flower,
the growth of a child,
a marriage that lasts.

I do not know how these things happen —
where that blaze of fire in the sky started,
what compelled that plant to bloom,
what turned that tiny baby into a woman,
why you stayed with me all these years.

I do know that these things cannot be rushed.
They happen at their own pace
and are seen only by those
patient enough to wait
and lucky enough to be there.

# Fog

Some mornings are very quiet.

Fog obscures color and detail,
muffles sounds,
keeps birds in their nests,
whispers "stay in bed."

It bathes plants and earth,
bejewels spider webs,
moistens rose buds,
silences footsteps.

Fog quietly delivers its message:
move softly,
love gently,
accept mystery.

# Fairy Dance

Sometimes light
dances on the water
like thousands of fairies
celebrating the wedding
of the sun and the moon.

Farther off shore
giant whales
spout white plumes
of hot breath
and sing for us all.

Constantly moving,
silently laughing,
fleet – footed revelers
remind us
to live and rejoice.

# The Coast

Nervous little birds
dart across the face
of a seaside cliff.

Endless waves
roll and foam
rattling the rocks below.

A black cat with no tail
stretches in the
sunlit garden above.

Life moves and sings
out of the great silence
all around.

# California Poppies

The poppies
on the face
of the rocky cliff
glow like a fire.

Their bright petals
are smooth and soft
like the lips of a lover.

Their thin leaves
are delicate
like fragile lace
made years ago
by the patient hands of wives
waiting on shore
for their seafaring husbands
to return from months
on distant seas.

The poppies
on the dry cliff
prove that sometimes
seeds fall
on rocky, barren ground
and thrive,
surviving
because of their pure
love of life.

# Sunflowers

Sunflowers are the giants of the garden.
They watch the movement of the field mouse
and the flight of the sparrow.
They breathe the heavy perfume
of the honeysuckle and jasmine.
They hear the hum of the bee
and the soft singing of the gardener.

They know more than all the other plants
in the summer garden.
This knowledge, turning into wisdom,
makes them bow their massive heads.

# She Likes to Knit

My wife likes to knit.
She says it is relaxing.

She has made
scarves, sweaters, and shawls.

Today she is bringing
blue, white, and tan yarns
together in thin lines
like those places
where endless waves
wash upon
endless grains of sand.

I think she knits
to relax,
to bring order
to undisciplined threads,
and to create
beautiful things
that contain her love
when she gives them away.

# Moonlight

She likes to see
the full moon rise,
silver or amber,

to see that faint color
in the night sky
before the first arc
of intense light
peeks above the horizon,

to stand in awe
of Nature's quiet beauty
and repetitive generosity.

I like to share
those moments with her,
not so much to see
that bright disc in the sky
or its light
on the land or water,

but to see
its light on her face
illuminating the beauty
that is there today
and reminding me
of the first time
I saw her smile.

# Now

Some people
spend a lot of time
thinking about Eternity
when moments will dissolve
into one unending
stream of consciousness

but I like to think
about Now.
I mean this moment
or maybe the next,
with this color in the sky,
this scent in the wind,
this hand on my shoulder

and the Now
when your breasts
are near my face,

your nakedness
meets mine,
and we make time
dissolve.

I like to think
about the thousands of Nows
that might occur
before I have to think about
Eternity.

# Meditating

The young monk
sat for hours
trying to quiet
the monkey in the mind.
He sought to experience
Nothing.

He felt and thought
without relief
while I held a pen,
stared at blank paper,
and could think only of
Nothing.

He could not escape
the aches in his back,
the sound of his father's voice,
the smell of new cut grass.

# Layers

Scientists call it
sedimentary rock,
the product of patient settling
onto the ocean floor
where time and pressure
push silt and particles together
until they let go of their individuality
and become part of vast sheets of stone
layered one on top of the other.

Here, at the foot of a cliff
on the edge of a continent,
those multihued layers
do not rest horizontally
as they were formed.

They point straight up
toward the heavens
as if in prayer or meditation
trying to forget
the rage and wrath
that wrenched them
from the sleepy ocean bed.

I sit on a water worn boulder,
too full of doubt to pray,
too restless to meditate,
trying to remember
the songs my mother sang
when I was a child.

# Sand and Pebbles

Unyielding boulders
make the water
twist and tumble
as it travels
from the mountains
to the sea.

In quiet pools
along the stream
sand and smooth pebbles
silently bear witness
to the wisdom of the water,
the power of persistence,
and the inevitability of change.

# The Wall

Smooth stones
freed from
mountainous boulders
ages ago,
rough edges
tumbled away
on the shores
of primordial lakes,
are once again
held together
by concrete

working as one
to form a wall
in a garden
by a pond
with green lily pads
and tiny golden fish.

# The Glen

The restless water
or some violent movement
deep within the earth
made a cleft in the rocks
ages ago.

Now, in that space,
green ferns breathe
the moist air,
redwoods stand
tall and silent,
a stream speaks
of distant snowy peaks
and caresses
the trout living
in its mossy pools.

I sat a long time
not knowing
what to say
about such a place

then I left
quiet and at peace.

# The Hand of Providence

Some say the hand of Providence
is always gentle and generous
to the righteous
but don't ask Job
or those hungry children
pictured in magazines.

It may be that the all powerful,
all knowing force that creates
and sustains all things
likes the hard beak of the vulture
and the soft mouth of the worm
as much as the silver tongue of the preacher
and the uneven voice of the poet.

Maybe we should experience
each moment
fully without fear or grasping
and have faith
in what we do not understand,
hope about tomorrow,
and love for the lowly
and the lofty.

# The Seeker

He was only a guest
at the Hermitage
but he felt welcome
listening for the voice of God
among the hymns
and chants of the monks,
looking for the face of God
in the incense filled air
above the granite altar,
watching for the hand of God
moving clouds and fog
over the vast ocean.

He was comfortable sitting
in chapel, at table,
and on a wooden bench.

He saw light play
on the ocean and mountains
a hawk suspended
in a cloudless sky,
a mouse and scuttling lizards.

He was never sure
he heard or saw
God but he tried
and two weeks later
he did stop his car
and place a blanket
next to a man
on the sidewalk
sleeping
under a piece of cardboard.

# This Life

The bookstore shelves
are full of books
about past lives
and out of body experiences.

How lucky those authors
must be
to know so much
and have lived so long.

I struggle each day
hardly able to live
this life
and experience this body.

Maybe tomorrow
I will look in the mirror
and see
Julius Caesar or St. Francis

but today
I am content
to see a face
that simply needs a shave.

# In a Small Room

Once, in a small room,
I saw Christ.
He did not walk in
with a beard and white robe.

He walked in
with earth colored skin
wrinkled by years
working in the sun
on the farms
of California, Oregon,
and Washington.

He walked in
wearing tattered clothes
bearing the burden
of a serious illness,
and holding the hand
of a loving daughter.

He owned little.

I did not recognize Him
until He smiled.

Now I look carefully
at every face
and study every smile,
even the one I see
in the mirror.

# The Grandmothers Visit

The summer my sister was born
both grandmothers came to stay
at the same time.

They came to see the new baby,
welcome her to the tribe,
and help my mother.

One was rotund, jolly,
and called me Patty;
the other, lean, stick-like,
seldom called me by name.

Each had different ways
of doing things
and the thin, quiet one
went outside
to rehang the wet laundry
after the one who sang
while she worked
had done it
all wrong.

# Milk and Coffee

Do you like
a lot of milk
in your coffee ?

I mean
a lot of milk
the way Grandma
made it
when I was a small boy,
the way it would not
stunt your growth,

the way I make it now
when I want to remember
her face
and the joy
of her laughter.

# Grandpa's Pipe

Grandpa smoked a pipe.

He could hold
a six year old boy
on his lap,
pick up his pipe,
tap out the ash,
scrape the bowl clean,
blow through the stem
until it whistled,
open a leather pouch,
refill the pipe,

tamp down
the sweet smelling tobacco,
and light it with a match
all the while saying
you are a fine, beloved boy
without speaking a word.

# Well Worn

Most of my things
do not acquire a patina
even though I like
faded jeans,
well worn leather,
and the muted green
of weathered copper.

Maybe I wash my hands
too often
and touch the world around me
too little

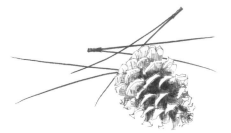

I remember outgrowing
a cowboy outfit as a child.
It was as clean as new
when we gave it away.

Time is making me
less afraid
of scars and stains,
more appreciative
of the hard and soft
people and things
around me,
more willing
to risk everything
to be well worn
and pleasantly used
before I outgrow
this life.

# Autumn

When autumn comes
and leaves change
from green to brown,
when chill enters the night,
when wrinkles creep
across hands and face
like weeds grown
in the summer sun,
when people no longer say
you look so young,
will I remember
the soft sound of spring rain,
the crash of thunder,
the song of a redbird,
the music of your voice?

# Distance

We measure distance
in so many ways —
inches, miles, light years —
and yet I do not know how
to measure the distance
between two people
sitting side by side
silent
or talking about the weather.

Hurt and history
keep them apart.
Blood and history
keep them together,
but always
between them is a distance
impossible to measure
impossible to ignore.

# The Hat

A stranger passed by
wearing a hat

an old man's hat
like my father's,
like the one
he gave me
for Christmas,
the one I wear
in the garden
to protect me
from the sun,

I do not look good
in that hat
but I am starting
to feel comfortable
in it.

## Untold Stories

The veins
on the old man's
thin arms
were like the blue
back roads on a map
of a lonely country.
The creases
on his face
were like canyons
carved by smoky clouds,
sun, and wind.

He called me "sonny"
and asked for a light.
I was too young
to care about his story
and he was too old
to remember.

# Sleeping Alone

It might have been coffee
with cream or maybe tea
with a lot of milk
in the cup on the table.

The kitchen showed
no other sign of use
and he remembered
leaving the cup there last night
before going to bed alone
as he had every night
since the day his wife heard
Dr. Phil on the Oprah Show say
"How's that working for you?
You don't have to take it
anymore!"

# The Blues

The music spilled off the stage
onto the audience.
Men and women,
couples and singles,
danced in the aisles.

The Blues Festival was more
about festivities than sadness,
more about a steady beat,
crisp guitar riffs, and a saxophone
that sounded like a lover
breathing next to your ear
than about someone and
everyone who did you wrong.

He was happy to be there
digesting a waffle cone
and a glass of beer
while he closed his eyes
and swayed to the music.

He did know sorrow and loss
but they were easier to forget
amidst that crowd
that loved the music
and applauded after every song
sensing that love scorned
can turn to hate
and sorrow set to music
can become joyous.

# The Fall from Grace

He did not know
exactly when it happened,
when he fell from grace,
when he was no longer
one of the chosen few.

Maybe it started that day
when he drove through a puddle
sending a sheet of muddy water
onto a man sitting in a wheelchair
waiting for a bus.

It was an accident
but he still laughed
and thought poor bastard
as he looked through
the rear view mirror.

Maybe it started years ago
when he was too busy
to change a diaper
or notice the smoothness
of his wife's skin.

Maybe it started only today
when he forgot
where he was going
and why he had gotten
into the car.

But it had happened
and he sat alone
in a shiny Mercedes
without a penny in his pockets,
without a hand to hold.

# In the Interest of Safety

In the interest of safety
I will be staying home today
thus avoiding the hazards
of highways, city streets, and bridges.

No disgruntled worker
will do me harm,
I will not be caught
in the crossfire
of jealous lovers.

Please pray
that I will not trip
on my way to answer
the phone or doorbell,
that a cookie
will not choke me
watching TV,
or that a rock from outer space
will not crash through the roof.

On second thought
I will be in the bar
down the street
or crouching under a bridge.
My nervous eyes
will let you know
who I am.

Please do not
approach me too quickly
or say Hello
until you are sure
that I am aware
of your presence.

# Fountains

I like fountains
especially in gardens
where the sound
of moving water
carries on a breeze
that stirs leaves and flowers.


Today that breeze
also carries the sound
of a distant bell
tolling to mourn someone

who also may have loved
the sounds of moving water
and the sights and scents
of a garden.


I do not know
his or her name
but I do know
the value of this moment,
the beauty of this place,
and the meaning of gratefulness.

# Ashes

When I die
wait for a windy day
and carry my ashes
to a rocky point
that juts into the sea.

Scatter those ashes slowly
to mix
with the air, water, and earth,
to become one
with the fishes,
the shore birds and sand fleas,
and the yellow flowers
that cover the meadow
every spring.

Years from now
listen for my voice
in birdsong
look for my face
among the leaves of the oak,
and know
that I move
in the depths of the ocean.

## After His Death

His depression lifted
and he fed the roses
growing over his grave.

It did not happen
the first year after his death
but it did happen

and the world was a better place
because of his generosity
and the beauty it produced.

# Beneath the Snow

During the darkest winter night
slumbering beneath the snow
seeds and bulbs wait
for the windsong of spring

that will awaken them
to sink deep roots
and send leaves and buds
toward the sun.

I know this to be true
not because I have
shoveled away the snow
or dug into the frozen earth

but because I have watched
the wheel of time
spinning on its axis
and because I believe

the ancient voices
that proclaimed
for everything
there is a season.

# We Only Need

We need not count
the seeds atop
the swaying grasses

or number the waves
rolling onto the rocky shore

or measure how far the eye can see
before the ocean vast
meets the sky immense.

We need not imagine
how many fishes
wander the depths

or where the stars reside
in the blue sky of day.

Nor must we be aware
of our hearts
pumping in our chests

or the movement of tiny sparks
in the neurons of our brains.

We only need sense
the One who creates
and sustains all things

and breathes when we breathe,
cries when we cry.

**When Sunflowers Speak**
*can be ordered through*
*your local book store*
*or directly*
*from:*

Pacific Grove Publishing
P. O. Box 803
Pacific Grove, CA 93950

Telephone (831) 755-1701
Fax (831) 375-4749

Email: pgpublishing@redshift.com